PLAYING BUSINESS GAMES

Featuring 12 commandments for
Managers and Business Owners to navigate from chaos to
mastery in Business

ANI SEDRAKYAN

DEDICATION

With immense gratitude,
I dedicate this book to my extraordinary family – to my mother,
Margarit Karapetyan, my father, Nairi Sedrakyan, my brother,
Hayk Sedrakyan, and his wife, Jane Sukiasyan.
Special mention to my cherished niece, Luna Sedrakyan.
Your unwavering support and boundless inspiration have been
the cornerstone of my captivating journey into the realms of
business and success.

CONTENTS

PREFACE

"Playing Business Games" is a valuable guide because it offers practical insights on self-management, effective leadership and business strategies. It empowers business owners and managers by providing actionable advice to enhance personal efficiency, navigate team dynamics, and optimize overall business performance.

The book serves as a comprehensive toolkit, equipping readers with the skills to thrive in both personal and professional aspects of their roles.

WHAT IS EXPECTING YOU AFTER READING THIS BOOK?

0.   Change of Mindset and Thoughts.
1.   Noticing the new viewpoints, games and reality in your life.
2.   Cleaning up not working habits and thoughts, that are "worn" and need to be changed for your best.
3.   Change of some habits. Some old habits will disappear little by little and some new ones will appear. It is because of the change of thoughts and mindset.
4.   After a month, 2-3 months or maybe half or in a year you will gain a harvest. The time depends on the speed and willingness of your subconscious mind. Usually, under harvest we see the communication and relationship upgraded, comfortable working atmosphere created, more confidence in your thoughts and doings, mature decisions taken in the business and personal life, income increased for several times, normally from x2 up to x10. Good things opening your doors.
5.   Upgrade of personal consciousness.
6.   Arsenal of the new interesting games, that will make you win by offering the winning conditions for others.

♥   **This is handbook is for You to play corporate and business games in a brilliance and mastery way and get what you deserve and want in your life!**

1 SHADOW CRITIQUE

KEY TAKEAWAYS OF THIS CHAPTER

You will understand:
- ✓ What is manipulation game of Shadow Critique. Why usually people play it. What's the interest.

You will enhance your skills:
- ✓ To reveal the manipulation.
- ✓ To overcome the manipulation.
- ✓ And of course, navigate the situation.

THE GAME

In the high-stakes world of corporate maneuvering, there exists a subtle game called "The Shadow Critique." Business owners and managers deftly wield blame as their weapon, creating an environment where employees feel the weight of guilt.

Meet Alex, a diligent employee at a design firm. The owner, Mr. Thornton, plays The Shadow Critique with finesse. He hones in on vague criticisms, repeatedly stating the work isn't up to par without specifying what needs improvement.

One day, during a team meeting, Mr. Thornton declares, "The quality here is lacking. We need to step it up." The room buzzes with tension as employees exchange uncertain glances. No one is quite sure what aspect of their work is falling short.

Days later, Mr. Thornton revisits the issue. "This isn't cutting it. Redo it, and make it better this time." The team, now grappling with uncertainty, dedicates extra hours to revising their work, trying to meet an elusive standard.

The Shadow Critique game is subtle but powerful. By maintaining ambiguity, managers keep employees on edge, constantly striving for an ever-changing target. It's a psychological ploy, pushing workers to overdeliver without clear direction.

In this game, blame is a currency, and guilt is the fuel that propels the workforce to toil beyond contractual obligations. The Shadow Critique isn't just about the quality of work; it's about manipulation, a strategic dance where the rules remain veiled, and success is a shifting mirage.

THE PSYCHOLOGICAL STRATEGY BEHIND THE "SHADOW CRITIQUE"

This game is to create a perpetual state of uncertainty and guilt among employees. By offering vague criticisms and maintaining ambiguity, the manager induces a feeling of inadequacy, compelling employees to work harder to prove themselves.

The manipulator's interest lies in leveraging this guilt as a tool for extracting more work without additional compensation. Through the constant sense of falling short, employees willingly invest extra time and effort to meet elusive expectations. This benefits the manipulator by maximizing output without incurring the cost of overtime pay.

In essence, it's a calculated manipulation that exploits psychological pressure, fostering a culture of overwork driven by the employee's desire to alleviate guilt and meet unclear standards. The manager gains both productivity and cost savings, creating a dynamic where the manipulator benefits at the expense of the manipulated.

The secondary interest for the manipulator is to control – in order to get what he/she wants.

Remember: when someone wants to make you feel guilty, they want to control you. "Healthy" and mature people do not play on the weaknesses.

How to understand it is manipulation?

When you feel angry it is already the signal. Usually, our subconscious mind gives us signals and wants to protect us. Feeling angry and anxiety is one of the symptoms of being manipulated. Meanwhile, do not judge only by 1 symptom. Always check with the check list. This is the method, that doctors use to make diagnosis.

Detecting manipulation can be subtle, but here are signs to watch for:

1. Vague Criticism:
If feedback lacks specifics or clarity, it may be a manipulation tactic.

2. Constant Guilt-Tripping:
Feeling perpetually guilty without clear reasons could signal manipulation.

3. Ambiguous Requests:
Unclear or ever-changing expectations may be a form of manipulation.

4. Lack of Transparency:
If information is consistently withheld, it might be a manipulation strategy.

5. Emotional Pressure:
Feeling pressured or emotionally manipulated is a red flag.

6. Inconsistent Standards:
Frequent shifts in standards without clear reasons can indicate

manipulation.

7. Isolation Tactics:
Manipulators may isolate individuals to control information and perceptions.

8. Guilt as Leverage:
If guilt is consistently used to extract favors or compliance, it's a manipulation tactic.

9. Gaslighting:
Denying facts or altering reality to create confusion is a manipulation technique.

10. Unreasonable Demands:
If demands exceed normal expectations without justification, manipulation may be at play.

Being aware of these signs can help you recognize potential manipulation and empower you to respond appropriately.

Manipulators think they are great psychologists and can play with the emotions of the people, control them and get what they want. Sometimes it is true, but not always.

HOW TO OVERCOME THE MANIPULATION AND NAVIGATE THE SITUATION?

Empower yourself with assertiveness:

♥ Clarity is Key:
o   Clearly express your understanding of the situation, seeking specific details.

♥ Set Boundaries Firmly:
o   Establish and communicate your limits regarding workload and expectations.

♥ **Empathetic Rebuttal:**
- ○ Respond to vague criticisms with empathy, seeking constructive dialogue.

♥ **Document Everything:**
- ○ Keep a record of communication to counter any attempts at misinformation.

♥ **Confidence in Competence:**
- ○ Display confidence in your abilities to counteract attempts to undermine your work.

♥ **Calm Assertion:**
- ○ Stay composed when addressing concerns, projecting strength and composure.

♥ **Propose Solutions:**
- ○ Offer constructive solutions to address concerns, showcasing your proactive approach.

♥ **Team Collaboration:**
- ○ Foster open communication within the team to collectively address manipulative behaviors.

♥ **Strategic Information Sharing:**
- ○ Share information wisely to counteract isolation tactics employed by manipulators.

♥ **Professional Development Focus:**
- ○ Channel your energy into continuous learning and skill improvement, emphasizing your commitment to excellence.

By employing these psychological techniques, you can navigate the manipulative situation assertively and maintain control over your professional boundaries.

2 LEGACY HOLDER

Delegate wisely – entrust each task to its masterful executor.

KEY TAKEAWAYS OF THIS CHAPTER

You will understand:

✓ The delegation is a Mastery. It is important to delegate. The most important is to delegate wisely to the matching person and in a SMART way.

You will Learn:

✓ Do's and Don'ts of delegation.
✓ The golden rule of delegation.

You will Do:

✓ Practice to assess capacity and skills of the people.
✓ Exercise "Delegate Masterful".

Welcome to the world of "Legacy Holders," where business managers cling to their past roles, reluctant to delegate. In this game, the fear of losing control and a belief in unmatched quality keep them tethered to tasks they've outgrown. Meet Jack, the CEO who still manages sales like he's the sales manager, unable to embrace his current leadership role.

The Legacy Holders game explores the challenges of releasing control, illustrating how this reluctance stifles growth and innovation within a business. It's a journey of breaking free from old roles, unlocking the potential for true leadership, and trusting others to contribute their expertise.

WHO IS LEGACY HOLDER?

A "legacy holder" refers to someone, often in a business context, who clings to their past roles and responsibilities, refusing to delegate tasks. This term highlights individuals who struggle to transition into new leadership positions, possibly due to a fear of losing control or a belief that others cannot match their proficiency.

Essentially, a legacy holder is someone who holds on to the practices and responsibilities of their past, hindering the growth and evolution of their current role.

THE STORY OF BUSINESS OWNER JOHN

Once upon a time in the bustling world of business, there was a well-intentioned entrepreneur, John. He believed in delegating tasks to ease his workload. However, John's downfall began when he assigned critical decisions to individuals not suited for the job.

The consequence? A chaotic chain reaction of errors, inefficiencies, and financial setbacks. John realized the importance of restructuring his business, aligning tasks with the strengths of his team members. This chapter explores how mastering the art of delegation ensures each task finds its masterful executor, fostering a harmonious and successful business environment.

In the intricate dance of leadership, the golden rule emerges – the Rule of Delegation. **A leader's strength lies not only in personal prowess but in the art of empowering others.**
The wise manager, the visionary at the helm of a company, understands the transformative power of delegation. It's not just a choice; it's a strategic imperative.

The Rule of Delegation dictates that to truly lead, one must share responsibility, trust, and authority.

As a manager, your task transcends individual achievement – it becomes the orchestration of collective success.
Delegation isn't merely assigning tasks; it's fostering growth, nurturing potential, and sculpting a dynamic, interdependent team.

In the chapters of effective management, the Rule of Delegation stands as a guiding principle, transforming leaders into architects of organizational triumph.

♥PRACTICAL EXCERCISE
Mastering the Art of Delegation for Top Managers

Objective: Enhance top managers' delegation skills to optimize team performance and foster a culture of empowerment.

♥ Step 1: Self-Assessment

+ Reflect on your current workload and identify tasks that could be effectively delegated.

+ Evaluate your team members' strengths, skills, and areas of expertise.

+ Consider the strategic goals of the organization and pinpoint tasks aligning with your team's capabilities.

♥ Step 2: Prioritization

+ Prioritize tasks based on urgency, complexity, and your team's competencies.

+ Identify tasks that provide growth opportunities for team members while contributing to organizational objectives.

♥ Step 3: Selection Criteria

+ Develop criteria to determine which tasks are suitable for delegation.

+ Consider factors such as skill match, learning potential, and impact on team and organizational goals.

♥ Step 4: Delegation Plan

+ Clearly define the objectives, scope, and expected outcomes of each task you plan to delegate.

+ Identify the most suitable team members for each task, considering their skills, experience, and workload.

♥ Step 5: Communication and Instruction

+ Schedule a one-on-one meeting with each team member to discuss the delegated task.

+ Clearly communicate the purpose, expected outcomes, and any specific guidelines.

+ Encourage questions and ensure a shared understanding of the task.

♥ Step 6: Empowerment and Support

+ Empower team members by granting them the necessary authority and resources to complete the delegated task.

+ Provide ongoing support and be available for guidance without micromanaging.

♥ Step 7: Feedback and Recognition

+ Establish a feedback mechanism to receive updates on the progress of delegated tasks.

+ Acknowledge and recognize successful completion, fostering a culture of achievement and appreciation.

♥ Step 8: Continuous Improvement

+ Conduct a post-delegation review to evaluate the effectiveness of the process.

+ Identify lessons learned, areas for improvement, and strategies for more efficient delegation in the future.

♥ **Conclusion:** By actively engaging in this practical exercise, top managers will not only enhance their delegation skills but also create an environment where team members thrive, contributing to the overall success of the organization.

DO'S	DONT'S
$ Clearly outline expected outcomes.	X Avoid delegating trivial tasks.
$ Communicate the purpose behind delegation.	X Steer clear of expecting perfection.
$ Provide necessary authority.	X Delegate with intention, not randomly.
$ Inform others about the delegation.	X Foster collaboration, not autocracy.
$ Know and trust your team's capabilities.	X Allow autonomy without micromanaging.
	X Recognize and credit the team for achievements.

Capacity and Skill Assessment Exercise: Unlocking Employee Potential

Objective: Identify and leverage the unique capacities and powerful skills within your team.

10 STEPS

1. Individual Strengths Discussion:

Conduct one-on-one meetings with each team member.

Encourage them to share their strengths, skills, and areas where they feel most confident.

>>>

2. Skill Inventory:

Ask team members to create a list of skills they believe they excel in.

Include both technical and soft skills.

>>>

3. Past Achievements Reflection:

Have employees reflect on their past achievements within the organization.

Discuss how their skills contributed to success.

>>>

4. Peer Recognition:

Initiate a peer recognition session where team members acknowledge each other's strengths.

Collect feedback on each individual's notable contributions.

>>>

5. Skill Assessment Tools:

Utilize skill assessment tools or surveys to objectively identify strengths.

Discuss the results with team members to gain insights.

>>>

6. Task Rotation:

Rotate tasks or projects to expose team members to different challenges.

Observe their performance and adaptability in various roles.

>>>

7. Feedback Loop:

Establish an ongoing feedback loop for employees to share their perceived strengths and areas for improvement.

Provide constructive feedback to guide professional development.

>>>

8. Cross-Functional Collaboration:

Encourage collaboration across departments or teams.

Assess how individuals contribute to projects outside their immediate expertise.

>>>

9. Training Opportunities:

Identify training and development opportunities aligned with individual strengths.

Invest in enhancing powerful skills through targeted learning.

10. Goal Alignment:

Align individual strengths with organizational goals.

Ensure that tasks and projects leverage the unique capacities of each team member.

Conclusion: This exercise not only helps uncover the powerful skills within your team but also fosters a culture of recognition, collaboration, and continuous improvement. Leveraging these strengths strategically can lead to enhanced productivity and overall team success.

 **GOLDEN RULE**

Never put off until tomorrow what you can delegate to someone else today.

Practical Advice:
Choosing the Right Person to Delegate Tasks

1. Evaluate Expertise:
Consider the specific skills and expertise required for the task.
Identify team members with a track record or knowledge in that area.

2. Assess Workload:
Examine the current workload of potential candidates.
Avoid overburdening individuals already handling significant responsibilities.

3. Match Interest and Motivation:
Gauge the interest and motivation levels of team members.
Assign tasks to those who express enthusiasm and a willingness to take on new challenges.

4. Consider Learning Opportunities:
Assess whether the task provides a learning opportunity.
Delegate to individuals who can benefit from skill development and growth.

5. Communication Skills:
Evaluate the communication skills of potential candidates.
Effective communication is crucial for successful task completion.

6. Team Dynamics:
Consider the dynamics within the team.
Assess how well team members collaborate and whether the task aligns with the team's goals.

7. Past Performance:
Review past performance and achievements.
Identify individuals who have a proven track record of delivering quality results.

8. Availability and Timelines:
Check the availability and timelines for task completion.
Delegate to someone who can meet deadlines without compromising quality.

9. Trust and Reliability:
Assess the level of trust and reliability with potential candidates. Choose team members who have consistently demonstrated dependability.

10. Encourage Volunteering:
Encourage team members to express interest in taking on new responsibilities.
Individuals who willingly volunteer often bring commitment and dedication to the task.

Conclusion: By carefully considering these factors, you can identify the right person to delegate tasks to, ensuring a successful outcome and fostering a culture of empowerment within your team.

3 TOXIC LEADERSHIP: THE SECRET WEAPON -RESPECT

KEY TAKEAWAYS OF THIS CHAPTER

You will understand:
✓ The reason of sin of disrespect. Illusion of respect.

You will see how much you lose:
✓ Consequences of disrespect.

You will Learn to practice and gain from respectful attitude:
✓ How to cultivate respect in your daily communications?
✓ The Story: The Respectful Master of Sales
✓ The Tale: The Sun and The Wind

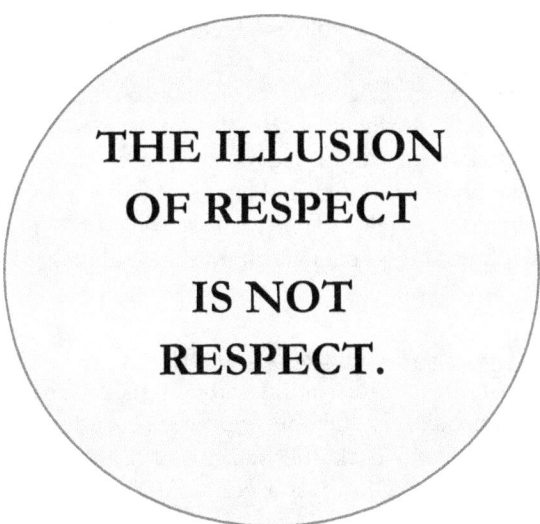

THE ILLUSION OF RESPECT IS NOT RESPECT.

Now we will Unveil the Mirage: Navigating Respect in Leadership

In the corridors of corporate dynamics, there exists a paradox – leaders who, though proclaiming respect, cast a shadow of insincerity through their actions. This chapter delves into the subtleties of detecting this dissonance between words and deeds, exploring the profound impact it can have on both employees and the overall organizational climate.

The Illusion of Respect:

In this section, we dissect scenarios where a top manager professes respect verbally but fails to embody it authentically. From dismissive gestures to neglecting the input of team members, the facade of respect unravels through emotional intelligence and astute observation.

Emotional Intellect Betrayed:

Explore how emotional intelligence becomes a silent witness, discerning the incongruence between what is said and what is felt. Instances of body language, tone, and micro expressions becoming the telltale signs of unspoken disrespect are highlighted.

The Ripple Effect on Team Dynamics:

Detail the adverse effects on the team and organizational culture caused by a leader's lack of genuine respect. A toxic environment, dwindling morale, and diminished productivity are consequences that resonate far beyond the individual relationships.

Navigating Solutions:

This section provides actionable strategies for leaders to align their words with sincere respect:

- ♥ Self-Reflection: Encourage leaders to introspect on their behaviors, acknowledging areas for improvement.
- ♥ Open Communication: Advocate for transparent and open dialogue between leaders and employees to address concerns.
- ♥ Leadership Development: Invest in ongoing leadership development programs that emphasize authentic leadership and respect.

Cultivating a Culture of Genuine Respect:

The final part of the chapter outlines the steps towards fostering an organizational culture built on authentic respect. From leadership training initiatives to instituting feedback mechanisms, the goal is to create an environment where respect is not just a verbal pledge but an intrinsic part of leadership DNA.

"Unveiling the Mirage" is a call to action for businessmen, top managers and leaders to bridge the gap between proclaimed respect and genuine, actionable respect. By navigating this delicate balance, organizations can cultivate a culture where every team member feels valued and contributes to their full potential.

THE STORY ABOUT CONSTANT FLOW OF EMPLOYEES

Introducing "Corporate Exodus," where a tyrannical businessman drives away talent with his disrespectful behavior.

Meet Richard Steele, the owner who values power over respect. His abrasive management style triggers a constant flow of employees out the door.

The game unfolds as Richard struggles to retain a cohesive team, unaware that his lack of consideration is the root cause.

"Corporate Exodus" explores the consequences of toxic leadership and the journey toward building a workplace culture based on mutual respect and collaboration.

When a businessman or a manager consistently lacks respect for their employees and disregards the importance of a positive workplace culture, several detrimental consequences may unfold:

1. High Employee Turnover:
Employees are likely to leave the organization due to dissatisfaction, leading to increased recruitment and training costs.

2. Decreased Productivity:
A lack of respect can demotivate employees, resulting in reduced productivity and hindered overall business performance.

3. Negative Reputation:
Word spreads quickly in professional circles. A business known for disrespecting its employees can damage its reputation, making it challenging to attract top talent.

4. Legal Consequences:
Unfair treatment may lead to legal issues, with employees having grounds to file complaints or lawsuits against the business.

5. Innovation Stagnation:

A hostile work environment discourages creativity and innovation, hindering the company's ability to adapt and thrive in a competitive market.

6. Poor Employee Engagement:

Lack of respect can result in disengaged employees who are less likely to contribute their best efforts or go the extra mile for the company.

7. Difficulty Attracting Talent:

Businesses with a reputation for poor treatment struggle to attract top-tier talent, limiting their potential for growth and success.

8. Negative Impact on Leadership:

The leader's own reputation suffers, making it challenging to form effective partnerships or collaborations within the industry.

9. Erosion of Company Culture:

A toxic atmosphere erodes the company's culture, making it difficult to establish a positive, collaborative, and innovative working environment.

10. Financial Loss:

Ultimately, the continuous loss of skilled employees, decreased productivity, and damaged reputation can result in significant financial losses for the business.

In essence, a lack of respect within a business or manager not only affects the immediate work environment but has far-reaching consequences that can impact the overall success and sustainability of the enterprise. Fostering a culture of respect is not just a moral imperative; it's a strategic investment in the long-term health and prosperity of the business.

THE STORY OF VICTORIA

Meet Victoria, a CEO who transformed her company through a culture of respect. Instead of berating employees, Victoria actively listened to their ideas, acknowledging their contributions. She implemented open communication channels, ensuring everyone felt heard.

Recognizing the importance of work-life balance, Victoria introduced flexible schedules, reducing stress and boosting morale. Employee well-being became a priority, with initiatives like wellness programs and mental health support.

This respectful approach led to a remarkable uptick in productivity and innovation. Employees felt valued, resulting in lower turnover rates and heightened job satisfaction. Victoria's success story in fostering a culture of respect became a beacon for other businesses, demonstrating that genuine appreciation for employees fuels both individual and collective success.

> # How to foster a culture of respect as a business owner or manager towards your employees?
> # Consider the following actions.

1. Active Listening:

Take the time to actively listen to your employees. Show genuine interest in their ideas, concerns, and feedback.

2. Open Communication:

Create an environment where open and transparent communication is encouraged. Foster a culture where employees feel comfortable expressing their thoughts.

3. Recognition and Appreciation:

Regularly acknowledge and appreciate the efforts and contributions of your employees. Recognize their achievements publicly.

4. Empowerment:

- Empower employees by entrusting them with responsibilities. Provide opportunities for professional growth and skill development.

5. Fair Treatment:

- Ensure fairness in all aspects of the workplace, from decision-making to resource allocation. Treat each employee with impartiality and consistency.

6. Constructive Feedback:

- Provide constructive feedback that focuses on improvement rather than criticism. Offer guidance and support to help employees grow.

7. Work-Life Balance:

- Promote a healthy work-life balance. Recognize the importance of personal time and well-being for overall job satisfaction.

8. Conflict Resolution:

- Address conflicts promptly and professionally. Encourage a collaborative approach to resolving issues within the team.

9. Invest in Development:

- Invest in training and development programs that enhance the skills and knowledge of your employees. Demonstrate a commitment to their professional growth.

10. Lead by Example:

- Model the behavior you expect from your employees. Demonstrate respect in your interactions with others, setting the tone for the entire organization.

11. Flexible Policies:

- Establish flexible policies that accommodate the diverse needs of your employees. Recognize and respect individual differences.

12. Cultural Sensitivity:

- Foster a culturally sensitive workplace. Embrace diversity and create an inclusive environment where everyone feels valued.

13. Wellness Initiatives:

- Implement wellness initiatives that prioritize the physical and mental well-being of your employees. Show concern for their holistic health.

14. Accessibility:

- Be accessible to your employees. Encourage an open-door policy that allows them to approach you with their concerns or ideas.

15. Team Building:

- Organize team-building activities to strengthen bonds and enhance collaboration. Create a sense of camaraderie among team members.

> By consistently demonstrating these actions, you contribute to a workplace where respect is not just a concept but a lived reality, fostering a positive and thriving organizational culture.

10 POWERFUL QUOTES

These powerful quotes emphasize the importance of respect in various aspects of life and relationships

1. "Respect for ourselves guides our morals, respect for others guides our manners." - Laurence Sterne

2. "I speak to everyone in the same way, whether he is the garbage man or the president of the university." - Albert Einstein

3. "Respect is how to treat everyone, not just those you want to impress." - Richard Branson

4. "Respect is a two-way street, if you want to get it, you've got to give it." - R.G. Risch

5. "To get down to the quick of it, respect motivates me – not success." - Hugh Jackman

6. "I'm not concerned with your liking or disliking me... All I ask is that you respect me as a human being." - Jackie Robinson

7. "Respect is what we owe; love, what we give." - Philip James Bailey

8. "Respect is earned, honesty is appreciated, trust is gained, and loyalty is returned." - Unknown

9. "Give to every other human being every right that you claim for yourself." - Thomas Paine

10. "The truest form of respect is actually listening to what another has to

say." - Bryant H. McGill

THE STORY
The Respectful Maestro of Sales
It's a true story from the experience of the Author.
The name of Sales Manager is changed for the reasons of privacy.

Once upon a time in the bustling world of sales, there was a man named Alex who transformed the ordinary into the extraordinary through a single, powerful trait – respect. His journey through the competitive landscape of sales showcased the profound impact of genuine regard for others.

The Humble Beginning:
Alex started as a novice in the sales arena, armed not with aggressive tactics but with a genuine interest in people. He believed in treating each customer, team member, and employer as if they were royalty.

The Secret Weapon - Respect:
In a world where pushy sales techniques were the norm, Alex stood out by treating everyone with dignity. He recognized that each interaction was an opportunity to build a connection rather than merely close a deal. His genuine interest in understanding the needs and preferences of his

customers set the stage for a remarkable transformation.

The Ripple Effect:
As Alex's reputation for respect spread, customers began to view him not just as a salesperson but as a trusted advisor. Word of mouth became his most powerful marketing tool, creating a ripple effect that extended beyond individual transactions.

The Empowered Team:
Within the company, Alex's influence was equally transformative. He treated his colleagues with the same respect he afforded customers. His team felt valued, heard, and motivated to excel. This harmony within the team translated into a synergy that propelled the entire sales department forward.

Sales Excellence Unleashed:
The astonishing result was not just increased sales but a loyal customer base that returned, not just for products but for the unparalleled experience of being respected and valued. Alex became the maestro orchestrating symphonies of success, all guided by the baton of respect.

The Grand Finale:
As the chapter unfolds, Alex's story serves as a testament to the profound impact of respect in the world of sales. His approach didn't just lead to high sales figures; it cultivated a culture of trust, loyalty, and excellence.

Key Takeaways:
- ♥ Respect as the cornerstone of effective salesmanship.
- ♥ The transformative power of treating customers, colleagues, and employers with dignity.
- ♥ Building long-term success through genuine connections and trust.

In the realm of sales, Alex's legacy endured as a reminder that respect isn't just a virtue; it's a strategy that can turn even the toughest leads into devoted patrons of the kingdom of quality service.

THE TALE
THE SUN AND THE WIND

The source of the photo: https://dzen.ru/a/XIdHwSlQewCzvP9O

Once upon a time, the wind and the sun decided to have a friendly competition to determine who was stronger. They spotted a passerby, and each took their turn trying to make him do something.

The wind went first, blowing with all its might, trying to force the man to take off his coat. However, the stronger the wind blew, the tighter the man held onto his coat, shivering in the gusty breeze.

Then it was the sun's turn. With a gentle warmth, the sun beamed down on the man. Feeling the sun's rays, he gradually became more comfortable, and, before long, willingly took off his coat to enjoy the warmth.

In this tale, the sun's gentle warmth triumphed over the forceful wind, teaching us that sometimes, kindness and warmth are more powerful than sheer strength.

<u>Conclusion</u>: people blossom from love and smile.

<u>To do</u>: Cultivate respect to make them feel loved and smile.

4 BLAMING BLITZ: TRANSFORMING BLAME INTO BRILLIANCE

Blaming Blitz: Unraveling the Psychological Game

In "Blaming Blitz," players engage in a strategic dance of shifting blame to shield themselves from accountability. The game thrives on sowing discord, leaving a trail of negativity in its wake. But why do they play?

Psychological Algorithms:

1. Ego Defense Mechanism:

Players deflect blame to protect their self-image, unwilling to admit faults.

2. Power Play:

Shifting blame becomes a tool for asserting dominance and control in the workplace.

3. Fear of Consequences:

Individuals fear facing consequences, using blame as a shield against potential backlash.

4. Manipulative Tactic:

Blaming others strategically serves as a manipulation tactic to divert attention.

Solution: Overcoming the Blame Game:

❤ **Cultivate Open Communication:**
Establish a culture where open dialogue is encouraged, reducing the need for blame-shifting.

❤ **Embrace Collective Accountability:**
Foster a sense of shared responsibility, emphasizing that mistakes are part of growth.

❤ **Constructive Feedback Mechanism:**
Create a system for constructive feedback, focusing on improvement rather than blame.

❤ **Conflict Resolution Training:**
Equip individuals with conflict resolution skills to address issues without resorting to blame.

❤ **Promote a Growth Mindset:**
Instill a mindset that views challenges as opportunities for learning and development.

❤ **Leadership Example:**
Leaders should model accountability, showcasing that taking responsibility is a sign of strength.

"Blaming Blitz" loses its power in an environment that values transparency, collective growth, and accountability. The antidote lies in fostering a culture where blame has no room to thrive.

Emotional Alchemy:
Turning Blame into Brilliance
in Business Leadership

In the dynamic landscape of business leadership, emotions play a pivotal role in shaping the organizational climate. This chapter delves into the art of emotional alchemy, where the transformation of blame into brilliance becomes a cornerstone for effective and inspiring leadership.

The Blame Game:

At times, blame can infiltrate the workplace, casting a shadow on team dynamics. Finger-pointing, negativity, and a culture of fault-finding can erode morale and hinder productivity.

The Power of Emotional Tone:

Explore the profound impact of the emotional tone set by a leader. The way blame is communicated shapes its effects. A constructive and positive tone can turn blame into a catalyst for growth and improvement.

Constructive Critique as a Catalyst:

Uncover the transformative potential of constructive critique. Instead of assigning blame, leaders can channel their energies into providing valuable feedback that fosters learning and development.

The Ripple Effect on Team Morale:

Analyze how a leader's emotional approach influences team morale. By adopting a constructive tone, leaders empower their team to overcome challenges collaboratively, creating a positive ripple effect.

Strategies for Emotional Alchemy:

- Empathy and Understanding: Cultivate empathy to understand the perspectives of team members.
- Positive Reinforcement: Acknowledge achievements and efforts before addressing areas for improvement.
- Solution-Oriented Language: Frame discussions in a solution-oriented manner, focusing on improvement rather than blame.
- Open Communication Channels: Encourage open dialogue where team members feel comfortable expressing concerns and ideas.

The Brilliance Unleashed:

As leaders master the art of emotional alchemy, blame is no longer a roadblock but a stepping stone to brilliance. Team members feel valued, heard, and motivated to contribute their best.

The Commandment of Emotional Leadership:

This chapter concludes with the commandment for business leaders: "Thou shalt wield emotional alchemy, transforming blame into brilliance through constructive communication, empathy, and a positive tone that inspires and uplifts the entire team."

In the realm of business leadership, the ability to navigate emotions and transform blame into brilliance stands as a testament to a leader's prowess, leaving a lasting impact on team dynamics and organizational success.

UNVEILING PSYCHOLOGICAL MECHANISMS AND REASONS *TOP SECRET* OF CRITICISM AND BLAMING

Psychological Analytics:
Understanding the Urge to Blame in Business Leadership

1. Defense Mechanism:

Blaming can be a defense mechanism, shielding the leader from acknowledging their role in a perceived failure. It offers a sense of self-preservation by deflecting responsibility onto others.

2. Fear of Failure:

Managers may resort to blame when confronted with the fear of failure. Admitting mistakes or shortcomings can be daunting, leading to a defensive stance of blaming others.

3. Control and Power Dynamics:

Blaming may stem from a desire to maintain control and power within the organizational hierarchy. By attributing faults to others, a leader may attempt to assert dominance.

4. Avoidance of Vulnerability:

Expressing blame might be a way for leaders to avoid appearing vulnerable. Open conversations about challenges and shortcomings can make them feel exposed, prompting a defensive response.

5. Coping Mechanism for Stress:

High-stress environments may trigger blame as a coping mechanism. Leaders overwhelmed by pressure might instinctively point fingers instead of addressing issues constructively.

6. Cultural Influence:

Organizational culture plays a significant role. In cultures that prioritize individual accountability over collaborative problem-solving, blaming can become the default mode.

7. Lack of Emotional Intelligence:

- Leaders with lower emotional intelligence may struggle to navigate emotions effectively. Blaming can be a result of an inability to understand

and manage one's own and others' emotions.

8. Insecurity and Low Self-Esteem:

Insecure leaders may resort to blame as a way to mask their own insecurities. Putting others down becomes a mechanism to elevate their own perceived status.

9. Fixed Mindset:

A fixed mindset, believing that abilities and intelligence are static, may lead to blaming. Leaders with this mindset may view challenges as threats to their competence.

10. Organizational Norms:

The prevalent norms within an organization can influence behavior. If blame is tolerated or even encouraged, leaders may adopt it as a means of conforming to the organizational culture.

> Understanding these psychological factors provides insight into the complexities of leadership behavior. It highlights the importance of cultivating self-awareness, emotional intelligence, and fostering a culture that values open communication and collaboration over blame. Leaders who grasp these dynamics can navigate challenges more effectively, creating a healthier and more productive work environment.

A STEP-BY-STEP GUIDE TO OVERCOME CRITICISM AND GIVE WISE AND CONSTRUCTIVE FEEDBACK AS A LEADER

STEP 1. Self-Reflection:

Begin by reflecting on your own emotions and potential biases before providing feedback. Understand your intentions and ensure they align with constructive communication.

STEP 2. Cultivate Empathy:

- Develop empathy towards your team members. Understand their perspectives, challenges, and aspirations. This creates a foundation for compassionate and constructive feedback.

STEP 3. Focus on Solutions:

- Shift the narrative from blame to solutions. Instead of dwelling on what went wrong, emphasize how improvements can be made. Frame your feedback in a forward-looking, solution-oriented manner.

STEP 4. Timely Feedback:

- Provide feedback in a timely manner. Waiting too long may diminish its impact, and addressing issues promptly demonstrates your commitment to continuous improvement.

STEP 5. Choose the Right Setting:

- Select an appropriate environment for feedback discussions. A private and comfortable setting fosters open communication without unnecessary pressure.

STEP 6. Positive Reinforcement:

- Acknowledge achievements and strengths before addressing areas for improvement. Positive reinforcement creates a balanced perspective and motivates individuals to build on their strengths.

STEP 7. Constructive Language:

- Carefully choose your words to convey feedback. Use language that is clear, specific, and non-confrontational. Emphasize your desire to collaborate for mutual success.

STEP 8. Encourage Dialogue:

Foster a two-way conversation rather than a one-sided critique. Encourage team members to share their perspectives and ideas, creating an environment of open communication.

STEP 9. Set Clear Expectations:

Establish clear expectations and goals. When team members know what is expected, feedback becomes a tool for growth rather than a punitive measure.

STEP 10. Recognize Effort:

Recognize and appreciate the effort individuals put into their work. This cultivates a positive atmosphere where feedback is seen as a constructive element rather than a punitive measure.

STEP 11. Continuous Improvement Culture:

Instill a culture of continuous improvement where feedback is an integral part of professional growth. Emphasize that everyone, including leaders, is on a journey of learning and development.

STEP 12. Training and Development:

Invest in training programs that enhance your skills in providing constructive feedback. Continuous improvement in your leadership approach contributes to a positive work environment.

STEP 13. Lead by Example:

Demonstrate the behavior you wish to see in your team. Be open to receiving feedback yourself, showcasing the importance of a growth mindset and a commitment to improvement.

STEP 14. Feedback Mechanisms:

Implement feedback mechanisms within the organization, such as regular check-ins or anonymous surveys, to create a culture of continuous improvement and open communication.

By incorporating these strategies, you, as a leader, can transform the feedback dynamic within your team. It's not just about overcoming criticism but fostering an environment where constructive feedback becomes a powerful tool for individual and collective growth.

5 PSYCHOLOGICAL TOOLS FOR *FOR DAILY USE* CONSTRUCTIVE FEEDBACK

1.
Use "I" Statements:

Express your observations and feelings using "I" statements to avoid sounding accusatory. For example, say "I noticed" or "I feel" instead of framing it as a definitive judgment.

2.
Focus on Behavior, Not Personality:

Address specific behaviors rather than making generalizations about a person's character. This ensures that feedback remains objective and tied to observable actions.

3.
The Sandwich Technique:

Start and end with positive feedback, sandwiching the constructive criticism in between. This approach maintains a balanced tone and ensures the individual feels valued despite areas for improvement.

4.
Ask Questions to Encourage Self-Reflection:

Instead of delivering feedback as a monologue, ask open-ended questions that prompt the individual to reflect on their performance. This engages them in the process and fosters self-awareness.

5.
Use Specific Examples:

Ground your feedback in specific examples to provide clarity and context. Instead of making broad statements, reference concrete instances, making it easier for the individual to understand and act upon the feedback.

These psychological tools emphasize empathy, objectivity, and a collaborative approach, creating an environment where feedback is seen as a constructive avenue for growth rather than criticism.

5 WEALTH WISE ODYSSEY: WEALTH NAVIGATOR

IN THIS CHAPTER...

YOU WILL UNDERSTAND:
- IT'S IMPORTANT TO MANAGE FINANCES AND LIKE A PROFESSIONAL FINANCE MANAGER.

YOU WILL KNOW:
- THE MAIN TERMS AND FIELDS, THAT IS MUST TO LEARN AND KEEP UNDER CONTROL.

YOU WILL BECOME
- MUCH MORE CONFIDENT.
- MOTIVATED TO LEARN AND EARN MORE MONEY.

In the mythical land of ancient Greece, imagine a business owner named Odysseus who embarked on a perilous journey, facing financial storms and turbulent economic seas. His wealth was scattered like treasures across distant islands.

As Odysseus navigated through the challenges, encountering economic monsters and unforeseen market tempests, he learned to harness the power of strategic financial planning. He sought the guidance of financial gods, representing wise investment decisions, and avoided the sirens of reckless spending.

Through cunning business maneuvers and leveraging the wisdom of financial allies, Odysseus transformed his scattered wealth into a consolidated empire. His wealth-wise odyssey became a legend, inspiring other business owners to embark on their own journeys, mastering the art of financial navigation in the "Wealth Wise Odyssey" game.

Building Your Financial Security Pillow

In the unpredictable landscape of life, having a robust financial security pillow is not just advisable; it's essential. This chapter explores the significance of this financial safety net and provides a practical step-by-step guide on how to build and maintain it.

Why It Matters:

Financial Stability: A security pillow acts as a buffer during unexpected financial setbacks, ensuring stability even in turbulent times.

Peace of Mind: Knowing you have a financial cushion provides peace of mind, reducing stress and anxiety related to monetary concerns.

Opportunity Seizer: A solid financial foundation empowers you to seize opportunities, whether it's investing, starting a business, or pursuing personal growth.

Step-by-Step Guide:

1.
Emergency Fund Creation:
Start by establishing an emergency fund equivalent to three to six months' worth of living expenses. This fund should cover essentials like rent, utilities, and groceries.

2.
Insurance Coverage Assessment:
Evaluate your insurance policies, ensuring they adequately cover health, property, and other critical aspects of your life.

3.
Debt Reduction Strategy:
Develop a plan to systematically reduce high-interest debts, freeing up resources for building your financial pillow.

4.

Investment Diversification:
Explore diversified investment options, spreading your assets across various classes to mitigate risks and maximize returns.

5.
Retirement Planning:
Strategically plan for retirement by contributing to retirement accounts and exploring investment avenues that align with your long-term financial goals.

6.
Regular Budget Check-ins:
Conduct regular budget assessments to identify areas for saving and optimizing expenses, directing surplus funds toward your security pillow.

7.
Continuous Learning:
Stay informed about financial management strategies and market trends, adapting your approach to maintain a resilient financial position.

8.
Professional Financial Advice:
Consider seeking advice from financial professionals to tailor your strategy according to your unique circumstances and goals.

Building a financial security pillow is not a one-time task but an ongoing process. This chapter aims to guide you in constructing a robust safety net, ensuring you are well-prepared for whatever financial journey life may throw your way.

The Wake-Up Call:
Lessons from the Pandemic

In the wake of the coronavirus pandemic, the lack of a financial security pillow left many businesses vulnerable to unprecedented challenges. Take the story of a small local restaurant, Bella Bistro, run by Maria.

The Scenario:

When the pandemic hit, Bella Bistro was forced to shut down temporarily due to lockdown measures. Without a substantial financial cushion, Maria found herself grappling with the harsh reality of unpaid bills, rent, and a workforce waiting anxiously for their livelihoods to resume.

Consequences of Unpreparedness:

1. Closure and Layoffs:
With no financial safety net, Bella Bistro had to close its doors, leading to layoffs and financial distress for employees.

2. Mounting Debts:
Accumulating debts became an inevitable consequence, with unpaid rent, supplier bills, and loan obligations looming over the business.

3. Inability to Pivot:
The absence of financial reserves hindered Bella Bistro's ability to pivot its business model or invest in online platforms, exacerbating its struggles.

4. Stress and Uncertainty:
The lack of a financial pillow heightened stress and uncertainty for Maria, affecting her mental well-being and decision-making during a critical period.

Lesson Learned:

Maria's story emphasizes the vital importance of having a financial security pillow. The absence of this safety net not only jeopardized the survival of Bella Bistro but also underlines the broader lesson that businesses, irrespective of size, must prioritize building resilience through strategic financial planning.

This chapter serves as a poignant reminder that unforeseen challenges can strike at any moment, and a solid financial foundation is the key to weathering the storm.

Your Financial Toolbox: Navigating Challenges with Ease

Alright, buckle up! We're diving into the nitty-gritty of finance management – you know, the real game-changer stuff. So, imagine you've got this toolbox, right? Let's call it the Finance Marvel Kit.

In this chapter we will explore the key tools managers and businessmen should be acquainted with while delving into the challenges they might encounter.

It's must for us Businessman, Businesswoman and Managers to know and practice the Tools of the Trade. Let's start from the very beginning. The terms can sound difficult, be sure it's very easy. The most important is to explore one by one and dive into the meaning. Afterwards, just practice.

In the wild world of managing money, it's like being on a treasure hunt. This chapter is your treasure map, guiding you through practical tools and friendly advice for financial success.

Practical Guide to Financial Management: Your Toolkit Unveiled

1. Budgeting Made Simple:

- ✓ **Start with the Basics:** List your sources of income and all your expenses. Be thorough; even the daily coffee counts.
- ✓ **Allocate and Prioritize:** Assign specific amounts to different spending categories. Prioritize essentials like rent, utilities, and savings.
- ✓ **Track and Adjust:** Regularly monitor your spending against your budget. Adjust as needed, balancing your financial ship.

2. Forecasting Without the Crystal Ball:

- ✓ **Study Historical Data:**

Analyze past trends in your business. Look at sales, expenses, and any other relevant data to identify patterns.

- ✓ **Factor in External Influences:**

Consider market trends, economic conditions, and industry shifts that might impact your finances.

- ✓ **Scenario Planning:** Plan for different financial scenarios. What if sales increase? What if there's a downturn? Be ready for anything.

3. Cash Flow Zen:

- ✓ **Create a Cash Flow Statement:** List all your sources of cash inflow and outflow. This helps you visualize your money movements.
- ✓ **Maintain a Cash Reserve:** Have a buffer for unexpected expenses. It's like having a financial umbrella for a rainy day.
- ✓ **Invoice Promptly:** Ensure you bill your clients promptly to maintain a steady cash flow. Follow up on overdue payments.

4. Risk Busting Toolkit:

- ✓ **Identify Potential Risks:** List potential risks your business might face – economic downturns, industry changes, or supplier issues.
- ✓ **Assess Impact and Likelihood:** Evaluate each risk's potential impact and likelihood of occurring. Focus on high-impact, high-likelihood risks.
- ✓ **Mitigation Strategies:** Develop strategies to mitigate identified risks. It could involve insurance, diversification, or contingency plans.

SIN OF THE MOST BUSINESSMEN
Using Business Cash Flow for Personal Expenses: Balancing Act

Meet Sarah, the proud owner of a small bakery named "Sweet Delights." Her business is flourishing, and the aroma of freshly baked treats fills the air. One day, a close friend invites Sarah on a dream vacation.

Case 1: Responsible Withdrawal
Sarah takes a thoughtful approach. She assesses her bakery's cash flow, ensuring essential expenses like ingredients, utilities, and employee salaries are covered. After careful planning, she decides to treat herself to the vacation without jeopardizing the business.

Lesson: It's possible to enjoy personal perks responsibly by balancing personal desires with the financial health of the business.

Case 2: Impulsive Choices
Now, imagine Tom, who runs a graphic design studio. Spotting a flashy sports car, he impulsively decides to use a chunk of the business's cash flow for a personal splurge. The business struggles to meet its financial commitments.

Lesson: While personal enjoyment is important, impulsive decisions can impact the business's stability. A balance is crucial.

Tackling Challenges:

1. Market Roller Coaster Fun:

Diversify Investments: Spread your investments across different assets. It's like having multiple rides at the amusement park.

Stay Informed: Regularly update yourself on market trends. Knowledge is your best companion on this roller coaster ride.

Emergency Fund: Have an emergency fund for personal and business expenses. It cushions the impact of sudden market dips.

2. Debt Demystified:

List All Debts: Make a list of all outstanding debts, including interest rates. Knowing what you owe is the first step.

Prioritize Repayment: Focus on high-interest debts first. Paying them off reduces financial stress in the long run.

Negotiate Terms: If possible, negotiate better terms with creditors. They might be open to adjusting interest rates or payment schedules.

3. Regulations Unraveled:

Stay Informed: Keep yourself updated on financial regulations relevant to your business. Regularly check for changes and updates.

Professional Advice: Consider consulting with a financial or legal professional. They can guide you on compliance and any necessary adjustments.

Documentation is Key: Maintain meticulous records. Proper documentation ensures you have the necessary paperwork for compliance audits.

4. Tech Friend or Foe:

Invest Wisely in Tech: Choose technologies that align with your business needs. Don't chase every shiny new tool; focus on what adds value.

Training for Tech Adoption: Ensure your team is adequately trained in using new technologies. Smooth adoption prevents disruptions.

Cybersecurity Measures: Implement robust cybersecurity measures to protect your business and client data from potential threats.

Short Story:
The Wise Restaurateur

In a bustling city, Alex owns a popular restaurant. When his daughter's dream college opportunity arises, he faces a dilemma. Through careful analysis, he reallocates a portion of the cash flow, ensuring both his daughter's education and the restaurant's stability.

Lesson: Strategic decisions can harmonize personal and business needs, fostering success on both fronts.

In these cases, thoughtful consideration of cash flow impacts personal decisions. Balancing personal desires with business responsibilities is key for sustainable success.

Smart Solutions for Success:

1. Data: Your Financial Sidekick:

Collect Relevant Data: Identify key performance indicators (KPIs) for your business. Collect data that directly impacts your financial goals.

Analytics Tools: Utilize analytics tools to interpret data. Platforms like Google Analytics or industry-specific tools offer valuable insights.

Data-Driven Decisions: Base your decisions on data analysis. It takes the guesswork out, leading to more informed and strategic choices.

2. Never Stop Learning:

Online Courses and Webinars: Enroll in online courses or attend webinars on financial management. Platforms like Coursera and Udemy offer a plethora of options.

Industry Publications: Stay updated with industry publications and financial news. They provide real-world insights into current trends and best practices.

Networking Events: Attend industry conferences and networking events. Learning from others' experiences can be as valuable as formal education.

3. Partnerships, Not Just Business:

Identify Complementary Businesses: Seek partnerships with businesses that complement yours. It could be a win-win collaboration that expands both your audiences.

Clear Partnership Agreements: When forming partnerships, ensure clear agreements are in place. Clearly define roles, expectations, and benefits for all parties.

Regular Communication: Maintain open communication with your partners. Regular check-ins help address issues promptly and strengthen the collaboration.

This practical guide is like having a friendly mentor by your side, offering straightforward steps to navigate the complexities of financial management. Use these tools, embrace the challenges, and steer your financial ship toward success with   confidence!   ...

6 MONOPOLY: PLAY TO YOUR STRENGTHS

IN THIS CHAPTER...

YOU WILL UNDERSTAND:
- PROS AND CONS OF HIRING RELATIVES' VS PROFESSIONALS

YOU WILL SEE HOW MUCH YOU LOSE:
- BY HIRING ONLY TAKING INTO CONSIDERATION 1 CRITERIA – THE TRUST.

YOU WILL LEARN
- THE SECRETS OF HARMONIOUS DECISION MAKING.
- THE STORY ABOUT A DOCTOR: BALANCING PROFESSIONALISM AND PERSONAL RELATIONSHIPS.
- DECISION MAKING PSYCHOLOGICAL TOOLS.

Enter Alex, a self-proclaimed chef wannabe who can't even boil water without setting off the smoke alarm. Yet, here she is, determined to impress her friends with a gourmet dinner.

As Alex juggles pans and spices, chaos ensues. The kitchen looks like a war zone, and her friends exchange wary glances.

Friend 1: "Alex, do you need help?"

Alex, with confidence: "No worries! I've got this."

Dinner is served. A peculiar mix of burnt offerings and oddly seasoned dishes.

Friend 2: "Is this... supposed to be edible?"

Alex, with a grin: "It's a culinary adventure!"

Lesson learned: When someone tries to play chef without culinary skills, laughter becomes the secret ingredient in the recipe for an unforgettable evening.

Lesson Learned:
Playing to Your Strengths

In the world of business, wearing the wrong hat can turn into a comical misadventure. Just as a chef shouldn't tackle accounting, a teacher might find themselves out of tune in the boardroom. The lesson is clear: Embrace your strengths, acknowledge your weaknesses, and let the right skills lead the way.

Conclusion: The Business Symphony

A successful businessman is like a skilled conductor leading an orchestra. Each instrument (skill) has its place and purpose. Trying to play every instrument can result in a cacophony.

So, don your conductor's hat, let each team member play their unique tune, and orchestrate success by embracing what you do best. After all, a symphony is most harmonious when each player is in their rightful place.

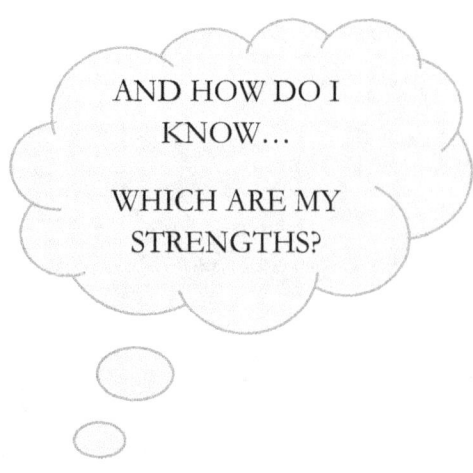

AND HOW DO I
KNOW...

WHICH ARE MY
STRENGTHS?

YOU MAY THINK
LET'S UNVEIL YOUR SUPERPOWERS

Welcome to the quest of discovering your strengths – the superpowers that make you uniquely remarkable. In this chapter, we'll embark on a friendly journey of self-discovery.

✓ Embrace Curiosity:

Imagine you're a detective on a mission. Ask yourself, "What tasks make me lose track of time? What activities spark genuine excitement?" These clues often lead to your innate strengths.

✓ Reflect on Feedback:

Think about compliments from friends, family, or colleagues. What do people appreciate you for? Their observations can be valuable mirrors reflecting your strengths.

✓ Passion Unleashed:

Consider your hobbies and interests. What pursuits light a spark in your eyes? Often, what you love doing is intricately connected to your strengths.

✓ Mind the Flow:

Recall moments when everything just clicked. That "flow" state is a treasure trove of strengths. Identify tasks where you effortlessly immerse yourself – that's where your superpowers shine.

✓ Trial and Error:

Don't shy away from trying new things. Experimentation is like trying on different superhero capes. Some may fit better than others, unveiling skills you never knew you had.

✓ Strengths Selfie:

Create a strengths selfie – a snapshot of your unique abilities. Write down what you excel at and what brings you joy. This evolving picture is your personal treasure map.

Conclusion: Your Strengths Adventure Begins:

Congratulations! You've just taken the first steps into the labyrinth of your strengths. This journey is about self-discovery, embracing what makes you exceptional, and unlocking the doors to a world where your superpowers fuel success. Get ready for an exciting adventure into the heart of you!

Now let's look on practical to do list. The ideas we do have. Now we need the to do list for all these brilliant ideas.

#1. Strengths Journaling:
Activity: Every day, jot down moments where you felt strong, capable, or accomplished.
Purpose: Recognizing patterns in your successes helps unveil your underlying strengths.

#2. Feedback Collage:
Activity: Collect positive feedback from friends, family, or colleagues. Create a collage of these affirmations.
Purpose: Visualizing the positive perceptions others have of you reinforces your strengths.

#3. "Flow" Exploration:
Activity: Engage in various activities and note when you enter a state of "flow" – total immersion and enjoyment.
Purpose: Discovering what activities naturally captivate you provides insight into your strengths.

4. Values Clarification:

Activity: List your core values – what truly matters to you.
Reflect on how your actions align with these values.
Purpose: Understanding your values guides you toward activities that resonate with your strengths.

5. Role Model Reflection:

Activity: Identify someone you admire. List the qualities you appreciate in them and reflect on how you can incorporate similar traits.
Purpose: Recognizing qualities you admire can reveal your aspirational strengths.

6. Skill Inventory:

Activity: Create a comprehensive list of skills you possess, both personally and professionally.
Purpose: Evaluating your skill set provides a clear picture of your capabilities and potential strengths.

7. "What Brings Joy" Exercise:

Activity: Make a list of activities that genuinely bring you joy. Prioritize incorporating these into your routine.
Purpose: Activities that bring joy often align with your strengths, contributing to a more fulfilling life.

Remember, these exercises are like keys to unlock the doors of self-discovery. Enjoy the process, and let the journey into understanding your strengths be both enlightening and empowering!

The Story:
This is where your strength lies

Once upon a time in the charming town of Serenityville, lived a curious soul named Maya. Maya had always been fascinated by the enigmatic concept of strengths – those hidden gems that make each person uniquely extraordinary.

One day, while strolling through the town square, Maya noticed a whimsical door that seemed to shimmer with an ethereal glow. Driven by an inexplicable curiosity, she decided to turn the handle, and to her surprise, she stepped into a realm of self-discovery.

This magical realm was filled with vibrant landscapes representing different aspects of Maya's life. As she traversed through, she stumbled upon the meadow of Endless Enthusiasm. There, she found herself engrossed in a creative pursuit, effortlessly lost in time.

Maya felt a surge of happiness, and an unusual energy filled her being. It was as if the meadow itself whispered, "This is where your strength lies."

In this enchanted place, Maya encountered the river of Unwavering Passion. As she dipped her hands into the sparkling waters, memories of moments where she felt invigorated and alive flooded her senses. These were the activities that not only fueled her spirit but seemed to infuse her with boundless energy.

The journey continued through the Forest of Joyful Accomplishments, where Maya discovered the trees bore fruits of achievement and fulfillment. Each fruit represented a task where fatigue was a stranger, and happiness was the companion.

With each step, Maya unraveled the mystery of her strengths. It became clear that whenever she danced in the meadow, sailed the river of passion, or harvested the fruits of accomplishment, time stood still, fatigue faded, and an exuberant energy surged within.

As Maya emerged from this magical realm, she carried with her the understanding that her strengths were intertwined with activities that brought her joy, boundless enthusiasm, and a replenishing energy.

Back in Serenityville, Maya began to align her life with these newfound strengths. The dance in the meadow, the sail along the river, and the harvest in the forest became not just activities but the compass guiding her to a life filled with purpose and delight.

And so, Maya continued her journey, each step resonating with the melody of her strengths, turning every moment into a harmonious symphony of joy and fulfillment.

6 MIRROR: PERSONAL REFLECTIONS IN BUSINESS

1st Key Principle: CEO's Influence on C-Level Managers

CEOs tend to hire C-level managers who share similar traits. The author's research on "Psychological Profile of C-Level Managers" revealed that hiring decisions align with the CEO's characteristics. Tests and profiles showed an 80-100% match between C-level managers and their CEO in a study of 40 managers, CEO, and Deputy CEO in a large organization.

2nd Key Principle: Mirroring in Business

The owner's personal traits shape the business atmosphere. For instance, an owner lacking discipline and organization leads to a chaotic business. The author suggests that instead of external solutions, owners should focus on self-improvement. A change in the owner's traits positively influences the business and the team.

Solutions for Positive Change:

Businessmen should prioritize self-improvement, fostering discipline and structured thinking. Encouraging the team to embrace these values creates a cohesive business atmosphere. Internal changes within leadership, such as open communication and self-reflection, are crucial. Instead of relying solely on external solutions, a commitment to personal growth positively impacts the entire organization.

Now, how can businessmen and their teams boost effectiveness and cultivate a healthy, constructive business atmosphere?

To enhance effectiveness and foster a healthy business atmosphere, businessmen should focus on self-improvement, emphasizing discipline and structured thinking. Encourage the team to embrace these values, prioritize open communication, and engage in regular self-reflection. Internal changes within leadership contribute significantly to positive organizational transformation.

The Reflective Mirror of Self:

In the quiet moments of self-reflection, we confront the essence of our skills and features. Are we effective communicators? Do we possess the resilience to navigate challenges? As leaders, these personal traits reverberate through the corridors of our businesses, influencing every decision, interaction, and outcome.

The Ripple Effect on Business:

Our personal habits and skills create a ripple effect in the organizational pool. A leader with strong communication skills fosters clarity, minimizing misunderstandings within the team. Resilience becomes the bedrock that transforms setbacks into opportunities for growth. This reflective mirror, when polished with self-awareness, amplifies positive qualities that echo across the business landscape.

Setting the Standard:

As leaders, our habits set the standard for the entire organization. If we prioritize time management and efficiency, these values permeate through every level. The mirror reflects our commitment to excellence, influencing the team to strive for the same. Your personal dedication becomes the cornerstone upon which a culture of success is built.

The People You Hire:

In the hiring process, this mirror becomes a litmus test for potential candidates. Are they aligned with the values mirrored in your own reflection? Do their skills complement and enhance the collective skill set of the team? The individuals you bring into your business should contribute to the harmonious reflection, creating a synergy that propels the organization forward.

Fostering Growth Through Reflection:

Reflection is not a stagnant pool but a river of growth. Leaders who embrace continual self-reflection become adept at adapting to change. This fluidity extends to the business, creating an environment where innovation thrives, and challenges are viewed as stepping stones rather than obstacles.

Cultivating a Reflective Culture:

Encourage your team to embrace personal reflection. Just as your mirror reflects your qualities, let each team member assess their strengths and areas for development. This collective introspection fosters a culture of continuous improvement, where everyone contributes to the evolving success story of the business.

Conclusion:

In the intricate dance of business, the mirror of personal reflection becomes our guide. It reflects not only who we are but also what our businesses can become. As leaders, our commitment to self-improvement becomes a beacon, guiding the way for our teams. Harness the power of this reflective mirror, and witness how the clarity it provides transforms both individuals and organizations on the path to enduring success.

Imagine personal reflection in business as honey. Like honey can be both a medicine and a poison, personal reflection can have dual effects. It all depends on how it's utilized. Just as improper use of honey can be harmful, misguided personal reflection may adversely impact the business. However, when employed wisely, personal reflection acts as a sweet ingredient, fostering development and growth within the business.

8 PUNCTUALITY AND SELF-DISCIPLINE: THE CORNERSTONES OF EFFECTIVE LEADERSHIP AND ORGANIZATIONAL SUCCESS

♥ The Time Paradox

In the bustling world of business, where punctuality and discipline are the pillars of success, there existed a peculiar character, Mr. Anderson, the owner of a thriving company. His mantra was clear – "Discipline is non-negotiable, and time is money."

However, the paradox lay in Mr. Anderson's own actions. While he sternly demanded punctuality from his team, his own track record was far from exemplary. Meetings meant to start at 9 AM often commenced closer to 10 AM, leaving his team stranded in a sea of apologies with clients and partners.

The irony reached its peak when Mr. Anderson implemented a policy penalizing employee for tardiness. Monetary fines were imposed, creating a culture of fear rather than fostering genuine discipline. The team, perplexed and disheartened, struggled to reconcile their leader's expectations with his own habitual lateness.

It wasn't just about the minutes lost on the clock; it was about the credibility eroded in each delayed meeting. The once enthusiastic team found themselves constantly making excuses for their leader, wondering how they could uphold discipline when their captain sailed on the winds of inconsistency.

As the paradox unfolded, it became clear that the blame game was not a solution but a symptom of a deeper issue – a leader who failed to embody the values he preached. The game wasn't just about being on time; it was a chessboard of trust, where each late move chipped away at the foundation of the team's commitment.

In the game of business, where time is a precious currency, Mr. Anderson's actions became a cautionary tale. The first lesson in this unfolding narrative: **leadership isn't about pointing fingers but about setting a consistent example.** As the story progresses, the question remains: Can Mr. Anderson break free from the time paradox and redefine the rules of the game?

♥

Time, Commitment, and the Essence of Discipline

In the intricate tapestry of effective leadership and organizational triumph, the threads of punctuality and self-discipline are woven with utmost importance. Let's unravel the significance of these crucial features.

The Punctuality Principle

Meeting the Mark:
Punctuality is more than just a habit; it's a commitment. When leaders prioritize being on time, they set a tone of respect for everyone's time. This foundational principle goes beyond mere clock-watching; it's about honoring promises and fostering a culture of reliability.

Words Weigh Heavy:
In the realm of leadership, the weight of one's words cannot be overstated. Punctuality ties directly into keeping one's promises. Leaders who align their

actions with their words build trust and credibility. The simple act of arriving on time transforms into a powerful statement about accountability.

The Domino Effect:
Being punctual creates a ripple effect throughout the organization. Meetings start promptly, deadlines are met, and expectations are clear. This precision cultivates an environment where efficiency thrives, paving the way for enhanced productivity and collective success.

The Discipline Doctrine

Self-Discipline: The Bedrock:
At the core of effective leadership lies self-discipline. Leaders who embody discipline exemplify a commitment to excellence. This trait extends beyond managing one's time; it permeates decision-making, work ethic, and the ability to navigate challenges with grace.

Leading by Example:
Leadership is a mirror. When leaders exhibit self-discipline, it becomes the blueprint for the entire team. This isn't about enforcing rules; it's about showcasing a standard that inspires others to rise to their best selves. A disciplined leader breeds a disciplined organization.

Resilience in Action:
In the face of adversity, self-discipline becomes a beacon. Leaders grounded in discipline approach challenges with resilience. This fortitude is contagious, instilling in the team a collective mindset that sees obstacles as stepping stones rather than stumbling blocks.

Creating a Symphony of Success

In the orchestra of organizational triumph, punctuality and self-discipline play harmoniously. When leaders orchestrate these principles into their daily conduct, they compose a melody that resonates across every level of the business. The result is not just timely accomplishments; it's a culture of responsibility, commitment, and unwavering success.

♥

THE STORY OF MARK AND DAVE

Once upon a time in the bustling city of Successville, there were two businessmen, Mark and Dave. Mark was known for his impeccable discipline, while Dave, well, Dave's chaotic approach was the talk of the town.

One day, a golden opportunity arose for both of them—a chance to secure a lucrative contract with the influential Company Royale. The catch? They had to present their proposals in just 24 hours.

Mark, the disciplined businessman, immediately dove into action. He meticulously organized his time, created a detailed plan, and set clear milestones. His disciplined routine included focused work sessions, regular breaks, and a good night's sleep. Mark believed in the power of structure, and it reflected in every aspect of his life.

On the other side of the spectrum, there was Dave. He saw the deadline as a distant speck on the horizon and continued his chaotic ways. Papers scattered on his desk, missed meetings, and constant interruptions were the norm. Dave operated in perpetual chaos, believing it fueled his creativity.

As the deadline loomed, Mark submitted a comprehensive proposal. His disciplined approach shone through, and his proposal was not only well-received but also impressed Company Royale with its thoroughness and attention to detail.

Dave, in the chaos of his own making, struggled to piece together a coherent proposal. The scattered thoughts and disorganized approach left Company Royale unimpressed, highlighting the drawbacks of a chaotic mindset.

The tale of Mark and Dave illustrates the benefits of discipline in business. Mark's success was rooted in his structured routine, time management, and attention to detail. His disciplined approach not only secured the contract but also positioned him as a reliable and efficient business partner.

The moral of the story: In the business kingdom, the crown of success often rests on the head of the disciplined. Structure, organization, and a clear plan are the keys that unlock doors to prosperity.

9 WHAT IS THE MOST IMPORTANT THING

Here you see the photo of Sunday Family Dinner, that Author adores and it is Family tradition from the childhood. It is one of the few most important things for her – The Family and time passed with loved ones.
All her partners know, that she is not working for Sundays, doesn't matter the income or any other reasons.

The Priority defines everything, where to invest your best time.

In the sunny capital city, where she grew up, a young author's journey began with a magical gift from her grandfather—a captivating book of fairy tales titled "What is the Most Important Thing" Filled with numerous short tales, each one held a unique story, leaving the young girl pondering the elusive answer.

As she immersed herself in these tales, the girl found herself puzzled, unable to pinpoint the ultimate importance. Years passed, and with maturity came clarity. She realized the tales weren't about a singular answer but rather a mosaic of values. Every reader, in every state of mind and at every age, perceived a different narrative.

In adulthood, she comprehended that life's book offered diverse stories, reflecting the unique values each person held. It became apparent that as we navigate life, we make decisions, choosing one path and forsaking others due to the limitations of our resources—time, effort, and energy.

Life, she realized, is a continuous series of decisions. The challenge lies in understanding our personal values, discerning what is truly important to us. In the intricate dance of choices, we allocate our limited resources, shaping our unique narrative. The journey is about discovering the most important thing in our world and investing our time and energy wisely.

♥

PSY TECHNIQUE "LIFE WILL"

Exploring the intricate balance of life, let's delve into the fascinating realm of the psychological technique known as "Life Will." Life Will is a methodology that helps individuals understand and navigate the complexities of life, uncovering the fears that often shape our journey.

Life Will is not a rigid set of rules but a dynamic approach that encourages self-reflection. It prompts us to confront our fears head-on, understanding that these fears play a pivotal role in shaping our decisions and influencing the delicate equilibrium of our lives.

One prevalent fear is the fear of failure—a nagging concern that we might not live up to our expectations or those of others. Another fear is the fear of the unknown, a hesitancy to step into uncharted territories. These fears, though often subconscious, act as silent architects of our choices, impacting the balance we seek.

The technique of Life Will prompts us to acknowledge these fears and gradually dismantle their hold. It involves introspection, asking tough questions about what truly matters to us and what fears may be preventing us from pursuing those desires.

Balancing life requires understanding that fear is a natural part of the human experience. Life Will empowers us to acknowledge these fears, dissect them, and redefine our priorities accordingly. It's a journey toward equilibrium, where our choices align with our authentic selves, fostering a sense of fulfillment in the delicate dance of life.

THE LIFE WHEEL OR BALANCING THE LIFE

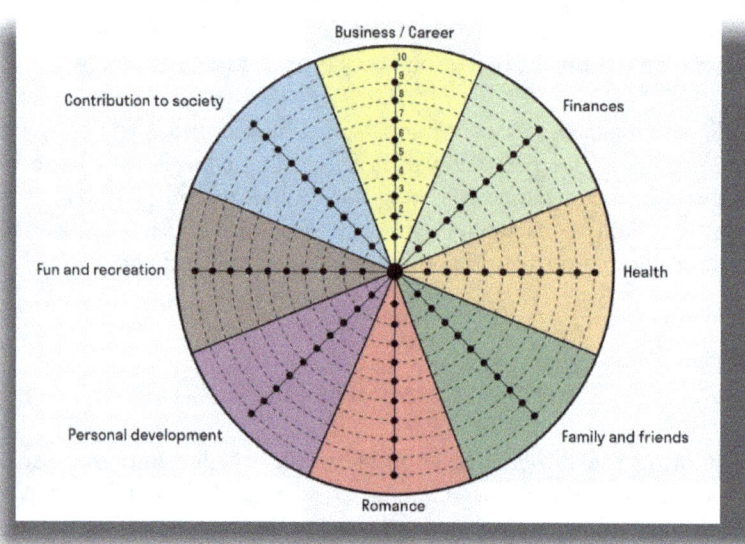

The Life Wheel psychological technique offers a structured approach to evaluating and enhancing various aspects of life. Divided into key spheres it provides a visual representation of one's current and desired state in each area. The wheel is usually made up of 8 categories or areas that are important for a whole or balanced life.

1. Business & career
2. Finance
3. Health
4. Family & friends
5. Romance
6. Personal development

7. Fun & recreation
8. Contribution to society

On a scale of 1 to 10, individuals assess their satisfaction or contentment in each field, creating a personalized diagram. This process fosters self-awareness, allowing individuals to identify areas where they may seek improvement or balance.

For instance, one might rate their current family life at 7 but aspire to elevate it to 9 in the future. The Life Wheel becomes a roadmap, guiding individuals towards setting realistic goals and priorities in each sphere.

By incorporating this technique, individuals gain a holistic perspective on their life, enabling intentional and balanced growth across various dimensions. It serves as a powerful tool for self-reflection and strategic planning, fostering a more fulfilling and harmonious life journey.

♥

Now, let's do together and you will do it for yourself after the example.
You put the date when you do your Life wheel and start to rating for the current moment.

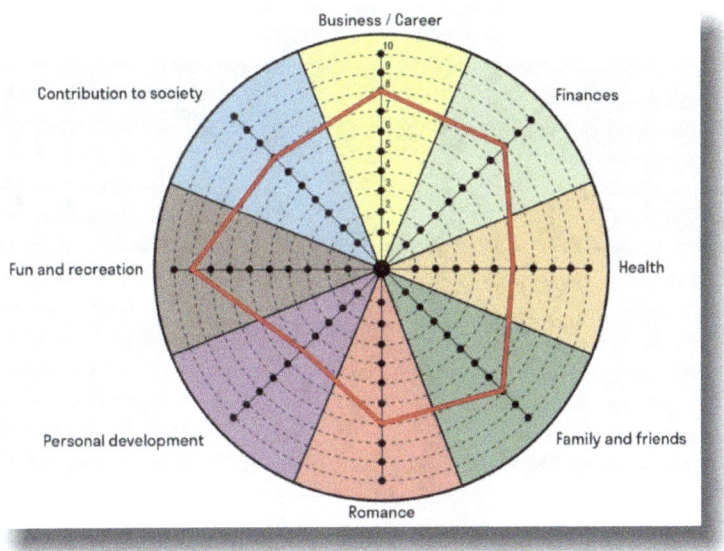

Ideally for Life balance is considered to have circle, all the categories in their maximum 10 grades. Hence, we are humans we can decide after 3

months, 6 months (the exact date you choose yourself) which enhancement or changes we would like to have it. On the same diagram #1 you rate first of all each category, then you join them to get future diagram you will be working on it. Better to do it by different color of pen or pencil, let's say red if prior was blue or black.

Afterward you turn the page and write step by step 8-12 things you should do to achieve, that new goal and have balanced diagram.

Remember to sign it and put the date and place, as well as write your Name Surname.

You should hang it in the very visible place, usually it is the bedroom to see it whenever you open your eyes or you sleep. These are the most powerful time in the day. Or you can prefer to hang it on the fridge, maybe stick it on the mirror of bathroom.

Decision is yours.

You should work on it and it should work for you and for your balanced Future.

10 PROFESSIONALISMS OVER RELATIONSHIPS

KEY TAKEAWAYS OF THIS CHAPTER

You will understand:
✔ Pros and cons for hiring relatives and professionals.

You will obviously see how much you lose by taking emotional decisions and working with relatives and friends:
✔ In this case you take into consideration the criteria you know them - you trust them.

You will learn:
✔ The secrets of harmonious decision making.
✔ The story about a doctor: Balancing Professionalism and Personal Relationships.
✔ Top 6 psychological tools for decision making.

Don't mix family ties with business. Build your team on professionalism, not blood bonds. Professionals come first. In business, choose colleagues based on professionalism, leaving no room for the influence of personal connections and blood ties.

In a business world where success is measured by results, every team choice is a fateful decision. There's no room for compromise between personal connections and a professional approach. Let's delve into this world of choices and explore why "Professionalism Trumps" is not just a slogan but a cardinal rule.

To start, it's not necessary to bring your relatives and friends into the team. Often, many share their success with loved ones, but in this chapter, I'll explain why such an approach might not be a blessing but rather a curse.

Professionalism is a key factor in team formation. When you invite professionals, you're betting on quality, on results. It's like hiring the very best, the coolest specialists who will take the business to a new level. Such an approach is the guarantee of successful development.

However, by involving relatives in the team, you risk upsetting the balance between personal and professional relationships. Honest and well-founded decisions may be questioned, and criticism may be perceived as a personal attack.

A beloved wife or husband, a trusted friend – it's wonderful, but it doesn't guarantee that their professional skills match the task's requirements. It's crucial to remember that in business, every team member must be a master of their craft.

In the following chapters, we'll explore how the right choice of professionals contributes to efficiency and success, and why "Professionalism" is not just a rule but a philosophy of successful entrepreneurship.

So why do business owners and leaders often include their relatives and close ones in the team?

Trust is an integral part of any successful business. Leaders, founders, businessmen aim for the team to be not just efficient but also based on trust.

It all starts with the idea of trust. When you bring your relatives into business, there's confidence that they share your values and principles. This creates a special atmosphere where each team member feels mutual trust.

However, there's a dilemma – how to strike a balance between trust and professionalism. We all know that there's no room for naivety in business. By bringing your close ones into the team, you risk losing balance if you compromise on professional requirements.

Navigating this dilemma, a leader understands that trust should not exclude professionalism. It's crucial for every team member, whether a relative or a hired professional, to be a true expert in their field.

When you choose your close ones, you place trust at the center of the business. But this choice also implies responsibility to ensure that your relatives are not only close but also professional partners.

Pros/Cons	+ Pros	– Cons
Professionals in the team	**+1. Professionalism:** The experience and knowledge of professionals guarantee high-quality task execution and outstanding results.	**– 1. Absence of Trust:** Establishing trust relationships is challenging at the beginning, impacting team dynamics.
	+2. Objectivity: Professionals assess situations without emotional influence, making informed decisions.	**– 2. High Costs:** Professionals demand high salaries, affecting the business's financial aspect.
	+3. Team elevation: Bringing the best specialists elevates the entire team's standard.	**– 3. Lack of Personal Connection:** A team of professionals may lack warmth and a personal touch.
Relatives in the team	**+1. Trust:** Family ties create an atmosphere of mutual trust and understanding.	**– 1. Lack of Professionalism:** Close ones may lack the necessary level of knowledge and experience in specialized areas.
	+2. Personal Connection: It's easier to maintain team spirit and motivation when team members are close in spirit.	**– 2. Conflict of Interests:** Decisions may be distorted by personal relationships, leading to conflicts and reduced efficiency.
	+3. Flexibility: Relatives may be more willing to collaborate outside regular working hours.	**– 3. Management Challenges:** It is difficult to establish a strict level of authority especially if you are both a relative and a boss at the same time.

In the end, the choice between professionals and family depends on specific goals, values, and business characteristics. Striking a balance between them can be the key to successful teamwork.

My Experience and Secrets of Harmonious Choice

My 21 years of leadership in top brands have taught me a crucial lesson – the harmony in choices. It's not just about separating professionals and family; it's about carefully considering how these two elements can jointly serve the success of the business.

The Secret #1: Unifying Professionalism and Trust
The key truth lies in creating harmony between professionalism and trust. Attracting professionals while maintaining a trusting relationship with the team is the true challenge.

The Secret #2: Understanding Business Goals
The choice between professionals and family should depend on the specific goals of the business. In which areas is the highest level of professionalism needed, and where is it essential to maintain a trusting atmosphere?

The Secret #3: Avoiding Compromises

Harmonious choices require avoiding compromises, not trust or professionalism. It's crucial to apply these elements in the right proportions to achieve a balanced and successful business.

The Secret #4: Creating a Unique Commandment

My experience has transformed into a commandment: "Success lies in the harmony of professionalism and trust. Choose so that each member of the team is a professional and feels like family."

Harmony in choice. Professionalism for success, trust for longevity. In every team member – both a professional and a family member.

6 Psychological Tools: The Pros and Cons List

1. Create a List:

Divide a piece of paper into two columns – one for pros and one for cons.

2. Brainstorm:

List all the potential positive outcomes (pros) and negative consequences (cons) associated with the decision you're contemplating.

3. Assign Weights:

Assign a relative weight or importance to each item on your list. This step helps prioritize factors based on their significance.

4. Evaluate Emotions:

Reflect on the emotional impact of each pro and con. Consider how each aspect aligns with your values and long-term goals.

5. Balance and Compare:

Review the lists, comparing the total weights of pros and cons. Assess whether one side is significantly stronger than the other or if they are balanced.

6. Decision Reflection:

Consider the emotional and logical aspects together. Does the weight of the pros align with your emotional comfort level and logical analysis?

Let's consider making a decision about hiring a person, exploring both a personal and professional version.

Personal Version - Candidate A:

+Pros:
+ Known personally, trustworthy
+ Good team collaboration
+ Shared interests and values

- Cons:
- Limited professional experience
- Potential bias due to personal connection

Personal Version - Candidate B:

+Pros:
+ Extensive professional experience
+ Proven track record in the industry
+ Strong network and industry connections

- Cons:
- Less personal connection
- Unknown personal values and team dynamics

Weights Assigned:

You assign weights based on your priorities, such as team collaboration, shared values, and professional expertise.

Decision - Personal Version:

After evaluating the lists, you might find that while Candidate A has a strong personal connection, Candidate B's professional expertise and experience carry more weight for this particular role. The decision might lean towards Candidate B for their proven track record.

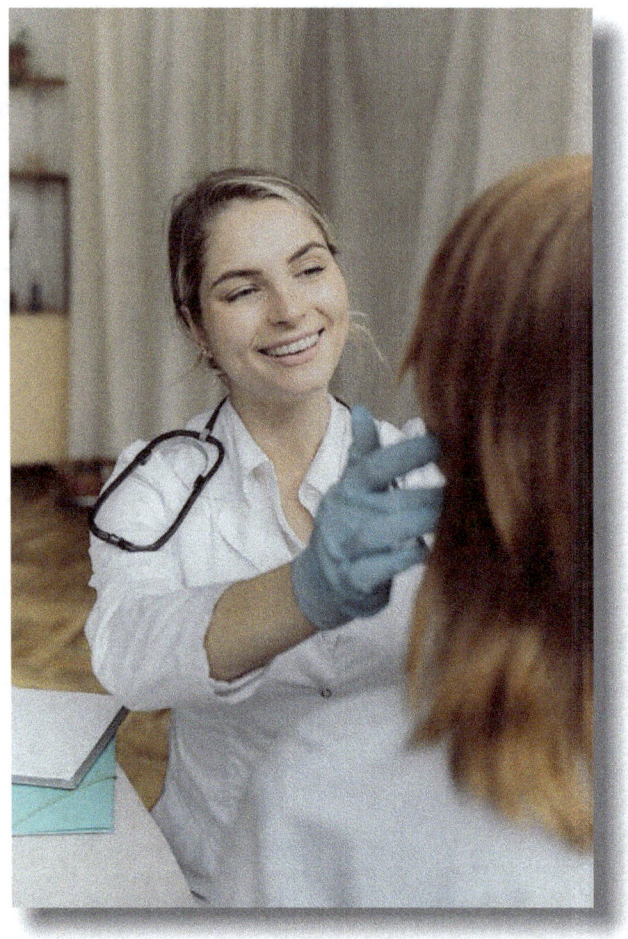

THE STORY
Balancing Professionalism and Personal Relationships

Dr. Sofia, a pediatrician at the hospital, faced various medical challenges every day. However, when her sister, Anna, sought her advice on childcare, Sofia was unwavering.

Sofia didn't just decline Anna; she firmly directed her to another specialist. Why? Because doctors are doctors, regardless of family ties.

She shared her perspective with Anna, explaining that professionalism, for her, is a sacred duty. Doctors, like therapists, deal with difficult decisions and balance on the edge of life and death. Redirecting her sister, Sofia emphasized the importance of remaining objective and neutral in her professional role.

This case reflects the principles of professionalism in medicine and therapy. Even in critical situations, doctors and therapists prefer neutrality to ensure a high level of care and ethical standards. Specialists make choices in favor of the patient, even if it requires rejecting close relationships in a medical or therapeutic context.

11 EXPERTS LACKING THE CONFIDENCE: DUNNING-KRUGER EFFECT

In the enchanting realm of "Zenith Esteem Trail," players follow the journey of Iris, a determined individual seeking to boost her self-esteem and confidence. Iris encounters mythical challenges representing self-doubt, societal pressures, and personal fears.

As Iris progresses through the game, she discovers empowering tools reminiscent of ancient artifacts. One such artifact, the Mirror of Inner Radiance, reflects not just her physical form but her strengths, achievements, and the unique qualities that define her.

With each level, Iris gains confidence points by overcoming challenges and embracing her true self.

The ultimate goal is to reach the Zenith of Esteem, a symbolic peak where self-assurance and high esteem reign supreme.

In "Zenith Esteem Trail," Iris's journey mirrors the transformative path individuals take to conquer self-doubt, showcasing that true confidence comes from embracing one's authentic self.

The game leaves players inspired, carrying the essence of Iris's triumphant odyssey into their own lives.

THE STORY OF SELF-CONFIDENT BUSINESSWOMAN SARAH

Consider Sarah, an aspiring entrepreneur with high self-esteem and confidence. Armed with a belief in her abilities, Sarah fearlessly pitches her innovative business idea to potential investors. Her self-assurance allows her to navigate challenges, learn from setbacks, and maintain a positive outlook.

In contrast, imagine Mark, who struggles with low self-esteem. Despite having a brilliant concept, Mark hesitates to present it convincingly. His lack of confidence affects his ability to communicate effectively, leading potential investors to doubt the viability of his idea.

The example illustrates that high self-esteem and confidence empower individuals like Sarah to articulate their vision, navigate obstacles, and resiliently pursue their goals. In both personal and professional realms, these traits serve as catalysts for growth, resilience, and overall success.

DUNNING-KRUGER EFFECT

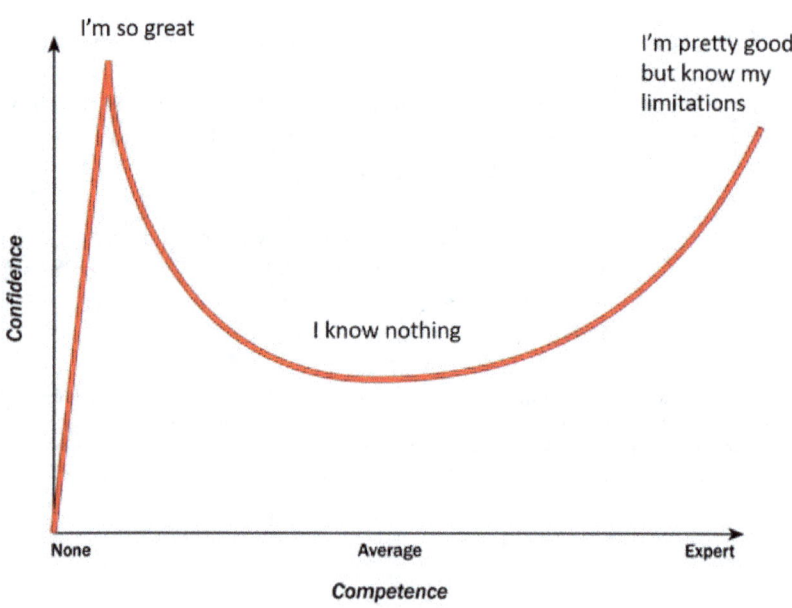

The Dunning-Kruger effect is a cognitive bias where individuals with limited competence in a specific area tend to overestimate their abilities. Coined by psychologists David Dunning and Justin Kruger, this phenomenon highlights a paradox: those with lower skills or knowledge often rate themselves higher than more competent individuals.

The effect encompasses several key points:

1. Unawareness of Incompetence:
People with low ability often lack the expertise to recognize their own deficiencies, leading to overconfidence.

2. Illusory Superiority:
Individuals with limited skills may erroneously believe they are exceptionally skilled, creating an illusion of superiority.

3. Misjudgment of Others:
Those experiencing the Dunning-Kruger effect may assume that others possess a similar level of knowledge or skill, underestimating their peers.

4. Recognition with Expertise:
Competent individuals, in contrast, tend to underestimate their own abilities and assume that others possess similar skills.

5. Learning and Self-Reflection:
Overcoming the Dunning-Kruger effect involves a willingness to learn, accept constructive feedback, and engage in self-reflection.

This cognitive bias underscores the importance of humility, continuous learning, and seeking feedback to accurately assess one's competence in various domains.
There isn't a widely accepted psychological theory that directly correlates higher intelligence with lower self-esteem or vice versa. In fact, research suggests that intelligence and self-esteem are not inherently linked. Intelligence is a multifaceted trait, and self-esteem is influenced by various factors, including personal experiences, social interactions, and one's perception of themselves.

It's important to avoid oversimplifying the relationship between intelligence and self-esteem, as both are complex and can vary significantly among individuals. People with high intelligence may experience challenges related to perfectionism or overthinking, which might impact their self-esteem. Conversely, individuals with lower intelligence may face different obstacles that influence their self-perception.

Psychological theories regarding intelligence and self-esteem are nuanced and context-dependent, acknowledging the diversity of human experiences and the multitude of factors that contribute to self-esteem levels.

Week-Long Confidence Building Plan:

Day 1: Positive Affirmation Ritual
Create a list of positive affirmations.
Repeat them each morning and night.

Day 2: Reflect on Achievements
Identify past accomplishments.
Acknowledge your strengths and capabilities.

Day 3: Visualization Exercise
Spend 10 minutes visualizing a successful outcome in a challenging situation.

Day 4: Power Pose Practice
Adopt power poses for a few minutes.
Observe the impact on your mood and confidence.

Day 5: Small Goal Achievement
Set a small, attainable goal for the day.
Celebrate your accomplishment.

Day 6: Positive Self-Talk
Replace negative thoughts with positive affirmations throughout the day.

Day 7: Social Interaction Challenge
Engage in a social setting, initiating conversations and practicing active listening.

Consistently incorporating these behavioral exercises throughout the week can contribute to a gradual boost in confidence and self-esteem. Remember, progress may be incremental, but each step adds to your overall sense of empowerment.

Here are 3 specific recommendations to help someone become more confident through challenging actions:

1. Public Speaking Challenge:
Recommendation: Participate in a public speaking event or join a speaking club.

Why: Confronting the fear of public speaking builds resilience and enhances communication skills, fostering a sense of accomplishment.

2. Skill Development Endeavor:

Recommendation: Choose a skill you've always wanted to acquire (e.g., coding, painting, playing an instrument) and commit to learning it.
Why: Mastering a new skill not only boosts confidence but also provides a tangible achievement, proving to oneself the capacity for growth.

3. Networking in Unfamiliar Settings:

Recommendation: Attend a networking event or social gathering where you don't know many people.
Why: Stepping outside comfort zones in social settings promotes adaptability and cultivates social confidence, expanding one's professional and personal network.

These recommendations offer specific challenges that, when embraced, can contribute significantly to personal growth and increased confidence.

12 READER'S GAME

Here will be added the reader's most common game.
Thank you in advance for your contribution. You can send your
proposals on Amazon comments or in LinkedIn.
The Author will gather all your stories and games, the most
commons and interesting games will be added in the chapter 12.

EMO SFIFT: POWER OF EMOTIONAL TRANSFORMATION.
TECHNIQUE OF
9 POSITIVE THOUGHTS-THINGS

In this chapter, the Author extends a unique gift to every reader—an invaluable treasure that transcends the material world. Within the pages that follow, you will embark on a journey guided by the author's profound insights into the "Nine Positive Thoughts Method."

Much like the author's love for non-material gifts, this chapter is a spiritual offering—a beacon of positivity, a catalyst for transformation. As you explore the pages ahead, remember that this isn't just a set of instructions; it's a gift carefully crafted to reshape your life, your mindset, and the essence of your being.

Prepare to receive a gift that goes beyond words, a gift that has the power to alter the course of your thoughts and emotions. The author, a giver of extraordinary experiences, leaves you with the taste of positivity—a taste that lingers, evolves, and becomes a lifelong companion.

May this chapter unfold a remarkable journey, and may the gift of the "Nine Positive Thoughts Method" be the catalyst for a profound shift in your life.
"Nine Positive Thoughts Method," where the author noticed a significant emotional boost by engaging in nine small, pleasant activities consecutively. These activities, like drinking coffee or calling a friend, are simple yet powerful when done in quick succession. The emphasis is on the immediate, consecutive nature of these positive thoughts to uplift and control one's emotional state over a short period.

STEP-BY-STEP GUID TO "9 POSITIVE THOUGHTS METHOD"

Here's a step-by-step guide for readers to practice the "Nine Positive Thoughts Method" and cultivate a similar mindset:

❤ **Start with Awareness:**
Begin by becoming aware of your current emotional state.

❤ **Identify Nine Positive Thoughts:**
Select nine small, pleasant activities or thoughts. These can be as routine as sipping coffee, enjoying nature, or recalling a happy memory.

❤ **Create a List:**

Write down your chosen nine positive thoughts to have a clear plan.

❤ Sequential Execution:

Perform these activities or thoughts one after another in a short period—ideally within an hour or two.

❤ Consecutive Focus:

Ensure the thoughts are consecutive, creating a positive momentum.

❤ Mindful Engagement:

Be fully present during each activity, savoring the positive moments.

❤ Observe Emotional Shift:

Pay attention to how your emotional state evolves during and after the sequence.

❤ Reflect and Adapt:

Take a moment to reflect on the experience. Adjust your list if needed for future practice.

❤ Regular Practice:

Incorporate the "Nine Positive Thoughts Method" regularly for ongoing emotional well-being.

Encourage readers to customize their list based on personal preferences and adjust the duration based on their schedule. This exercise aims to bring a positive shift in mindset through intentional and consecutive positive action

ABOUT THE AUTHOR

Ani Sedrakyan is a seasoned Business Strategist with over 21 years of expertise, having contributed her skills to 59 leading international brands. As the Chief Editor of 20 business magazines, she has left an indelible mark on the industry.

Her extensive services encompass a wide array, from designing marketing departments, recruiting teams, and conducting marketing audits to crafting comprehensive marketing and PR strategies. An adept media planner and budgeter, Ani excels in brand launches, marketing events, and campaigns, digital execution, analytics, and image development.

Ani's unique algorithms of development reflect a fusion of her rich experience and a robust educational background as a business leader and Marketing PR Strategist. Notable brands in her portfolio include Graff, Dior, Gucci, Dolce&Gabbana, and more.

Beyond her professional endeavors, Ani emphasizes life balance and continuous personal development. Her favorite quotes, "An investment in knowledge pays the best interest!" and "If you think that competency is expensive, try incompetence - it will cost you much more expensive," underscore her commitment to excellence.

For those interested in connecting with Ani Sedrakyan, she can be found and followed on LinkedIn at www.linkedin.com/in/anisedrakyan.